Y0-BFG-433

Exceptional
Children At Risk

*H*omeless and in Need of Special Education

L. Juane Heflin
Kathryn Rudy

Published by The Council for Exceptional Children

ERIC

A Product of the ERIC Clearinghouse
on Handicapped and Gifted Children

Library of Congress Catalog Card Number 91-58305

ISBN 0-86586-210-9

A product of the ERIC / OSEP Special Project, the ERIC Clearinghouse on Handicapped and Gifted Children

Published in 1991 by The Council for Exceptional Children, 1920 Association Drive, Reston, Virginia 22091-1589
Stock No. P353

This publication was prepared with funding from the U.S. Department of Education, Office of Special Education Programs, contract no. RI88062007. Contractors undertaking such projects under government sponsorship are encouraged to express freely their judgment in professional and technical matters. Prior to publication the manuscript was submitted for critical review and determination of professional competence. This publication has met such standards. Points of view, however, do not necessarily represent the official view or opinions of either The Council for Exceptional Children or the Department of Education.

Printed in the United States of America
10   9   8   7   6   5   4   3   2   1

Contents

Foreword

EXCEPTIONAL CHILDREN AT RISK
CEC Mini-Library

Many of today's pressing social problems, such as poverty, homelessness, drug abuse, and child abuse, are factors that place children and youth at risk in a variety of ways. There is a growing need for special educators to understand the risk factors that students must face and, in particular, the risks confronting children and youth who have been identified as exceptional. A child may be at risk *due to* a number of quite different phenomena, such as poverty or abuse. Therefore, the child may be at risk *for* a variety of problems, such as developmental delays; debilitating physical illnesses or psychological disorders; failing or dropping out of school; being incarcerated; or generally having an unrewarding, unproductive adulthood. Compounding the difficulties that both the child and the educator face in dealing with these risk factors is the unhappy truth that a child may have more than one risk factor, thereby multiplying his or her risk and need.

The struggle within special education to address these issues was the genesis of the 1991 CEC conference "Children on the Edge." The content for the conference strands is represented by this series of publications, which were developed through the assistance of the Division of Innovation and Development of the U.S. Office of Special Education Programs (OSEP). OSEP funds the ERIC/OSEP Special Project, a research dissemination activity of The Council for Exceptional Children. As a part of its publication program, which synthesizes and translates research in special education for a variety of audiences, the ERIC/OSEP Special Project coordinated the development of this series of books and assisted in their dissemination to special education practitioners.

Each book in the series pertains to one of the conference strands. Each provides a synthesis of the literature in its area, followed by practical suggestions—derived from the literature—for program developers, administrators, and teachers. The 11 books in the series are as follows:

- *Programming for Aggressive and Violent Students* addresses issues that educators and other professionals face in contending with episodes of violence and aggression in the schools.

- *Abuse and Neglect of Exceptional Children* examines the role of the special educator in dealing with children who are abused and neglected and those with suspected abuse and neglect.

- *Special Health Care in the School* provides a broad-based definition of the population of students with special health needs and discusses their unique educational needs.

- *Homeless and in Need of Special Education* examines the plight of the fastest growing segment of the homeless population, families with children.

- *Hidden Youth: Dropouts from Special Education* addresses the difficulties of comparing and drawing meaning from dropout data prepared by different agencies and examines the characteristics of students and schools that place students at risk for leaving school prematurely.

- *Born Substance Exposed, Educationally Vulnerable* examines what is known about the long-term effects of exposure *in utero* to alcohol and other drugs, as well as the educational implications of those effects.

- *Depression and Suicide: Special Education Students at Risk* reviews the role of school personnel in detecting signs of depression and potential suicide and in taking appropriate action, as well as the role of the school in developing and implementing treatment programs for this population.

- *Language Minority Students with Disabilities* discusses the preparation needed by schools and school personnel to meet the needs of limited-English-proficient students with disabilities.

- *Alcohol and Other Drugs: Use, Abuse, and Disabilities* addresses the issues involved in working with children and adolescents who have disabling conditions and use alcohol and other drugs.

- *Rural, Exceptional, At Risk* examines the unique difficulties of delivering education services to at-risk children and youth with exceptionalities who live in rural areas.

- *Double Jeopardy: Pregnant and Parenting Youth in Special Education* addresses the plight of pregnant teenagers and teenage parents, especially those in special education, and the role of program developers and practitioners in responding to their educational needs.

Background information applicable to the conference strand on juvenile corrections can be found in another publication, *Special Education in Juvenile Corrections,* which is a part of the CEC Mini-Library *Working with Behavioral Disorders.* That publication addresses the demographics of incarcerated youth and promising practices in responding to their needs.

1. Introduction

Families constitute the fastest growing segment of the homeless population.

Homelessness has traditionally been associated with being on "Skid Row," a term derived from Skid Road in Seattle, where indigents were known to loiter (Baxter & Hopper, 1981). This association conjures up stereotypic images of unkempt individuals who may be caught in the throes of alcoholism, poverty, and disordered cognition. Although this image may have been fairly accurate 40 years ago (Rossi, 1990), the profile of persons experiencing homelessness has changed dramatically. Now, the fastest growing segment of the homeless population is families with children (Rafferty & Rollins, 1990). The effects of homelessness on children can be devastating.

Before discussing the implications of homelessness in relation to students in need of special educational services, this book explores the magnitude of homelessness among families, provides empirical descriptions of homeless populations, and identifies factors contributing to the rising incidence of homelessness in the United States. Specific effects of homelessness on children and youth are considered. Chapter 3 discusses educational implications and documents federal programs that have been enacted to attempt to meet the educational needs of students who are homeless. Implications for teachers in relation to children with special needs and general teaching strategies are provided. Barriers to the provision of educational services are delineated as implications for administrators. Chapter 4 presents recommendations for program development and administration. Resources and contact information for programs and clearinghouses are provided in the Resources section at the end of this book.

2. Synthesis of Research

As many as 4 million people may be homeless, including 1.6 million children. A number of federal, legal, and social factors contribute to increases in the homeless population. Children are most susceptible to the devastating effects of homelessness.

Definition

Traditionally, homeless individuals have been described as people who live outside the family unit. In contrast, today's definition of homelessness describes an absolute inability to afford housing, which results in a dependence on shelters and other types of temporary accommodations (Rossi, 1990).

The Stewart B. McKinney Homeless Assistance Act (P.L. 100-77) defines homeless individuals as those who

1. Lack a fixed, regular, and adequate nighttime residence.

2. Have a primary nighttime residence that is:

   (a) a supervised, publicly or privately operated shelter designed to provide temporary living accommodations (including welfare hotels, congregate shelters, and transitional housing for the mentally ill);

   (b) an institution that provides a temporary residence for individuals intended to be institutionalized; or

   (c) a public or private place not designed for, or ordinarily used as, a regular sleeping accommodation for human beings.

Incidence of Homelessness

Although difficulties encountered in attempting to quantify the magnitude of homelessness in the United States result in discrepant figures, estimates are that there are between 3 and 4 million homeless individuals in the United States annually (Tower & White, 1989), or 660,000 homeless during any given week (Burns, 1991). Acknowledging that differences in reporting lead to incidence counts that err toward an undercount (Harrington-Lueker, 1989), the Department of Education estimated that approximately 272,773 school-aged children and youth are homeless (Cavazos, 1990). Of that number, 49% are elementary aged, 21% are junior high aged, and 26% are high school aged (leaving 4% unspecified in regard to grade level). In the same report, 19 states indicated the presence of 56,783 homeless children of preschool age. These estimates are considered low (Friedman & Christiansen, 1990). The Children's Defense Fund reports a much higher incidence of 1.6 million children who may be homeless every year (Burns, 1991). Homelessness among families increased 118% between 1988 and 1989 (Burns, 1991).

In addition to the individuals who meet the definition of homelessness as detailed by the Stewart B. McKinney Act, there may be as many as 14 million more who are considered "hidden homeless" (Linehan, 1989). The hidden homeless are individuals or families who live with friends or relatives because they cannot afford their own housing (Burns, 1991). Although these homeless individuals may have a fixed nighttime residence, living conditions may be less than desirable. Because conditions may be tenuous and temporary, hidden homelessness often leads to total homelessness (Rivlin, 1990).

Empirical Descriptions of Homeless Populations

Families are the fastest growing segment of the homeless population. Approximately one third of homeless people are members of families with children (U.S. Conference of Mayors, 1989). Recent studies indicate that the count may be as high as 52% (U.S. Department of Housing and Urban Development, 1989). One of every four homeless individuals has custody of a child (U.S. Conference of Mayors, 1989). The dramatic increase in numbers of families who are homeless is evident in an examination of the records for the New York City temporary shelter system. In any given month between 1960 and 1980, an average of 600 homeless families lived in shelters. In 1987, that number increased over 800% to 5,020 families per month, which included 12,303 children (Alperstein, Rappaport, & Flanigan, 1988). The average age of the homeless children was 6 years (Kozol, 1990).

The number of homeless families headed by single females may be as high as 90% (Stronge & Tenhouse, 1990). One study found that the average age of homeless women was the mid-20s; they had an average of 2.7 children whose ages ranged from 6 weeks to 18 years (Bassuk & Rubin, 1987). Bassuk and Rosenberg (1988) conducted a study in which the characteristics of women heading homeless families were compared to the characteristics of women heading housed families of similar socioeconomic status. Almost all of the women in both groups were single at the time of the study. Homeless mothers were more likely to have been battered by boyfriends and/or husbands, with 42% reporting abuse. Twenty percent of the housed mothers indicated that they had been battered (Bassuk & Rosenberg, 1988).

Ethnic representation among the homeless varies substantially by geographic region. In one study conducted by the Urban Family Center in New York City, 67% of homeless families were African-American and

24% were Hispanic (Phillips, DeChillo, Kronenfeld, & Middleton-Jeter, 1988). In contrast, a study conducted by the Child Welfare League of America (CWLA) in the cities of Washington, DC, Tampa, Detroit, Salt Lake City, San Francisco, Los Angeles, and Houston found that 46% of its homeless families were White, 32% were African-American, 17% were Hispanic, 2% were American Indian, and 3% were of unidentified origin (Maza & Hall, 1988).

Factors in Growth of Homelessness Among Families

Several changes contribute to the dramatic increase in the percentage of families among the homeless population. These changes include conservative federal administrations, a diminishing supply of affordable low-income housing, family financial crises, "no fault" divorce laws, and the rising incidence of runaway and throwaway youth. Each of these factors is defined and discussed separately.

Conservative Federal Administrations. The decade of the 1980s witnessed a deterioration of the services available to individuals who are homeless. Dramatic fiscal cuts in federal welfare programs reduced funding for Aid to Families with Dependent Children (AFDC), food stamps, and nutrition programs (Hope & Young, 1986). During the Reagan administration, nearly half a million families lost all welfare payments; a million people lost use of food stamp programs; and two million children were eliminated from school lunch programs. The Women, Infants, and Children (WIC) nutrition program is unable to provide services to even half of the individuals who meet their eligibility criteria (Kozol, 1990). During the 1980s, the federal government adopted the position that aid received by families in the form of federal funds must be considered income, and many families have subsequently become ineligible for food stamp programs (Mihaly, 1991). In 1990, a compromise was reached that allowed for only half of shelter costs to count as income, but families continue to lose other assistance.

Diminishing Supply of Affordable Housing. At least 23% of homeless families cannot secure shelter because of the scarcity of low-cost housing options (U.S. Conference of Mayors, 1989). Conservative government spending has led to continued reductions in appropriations for low-income housing projects, which has led to increasing shortages of affordable housing (Hope & Young, 1986; Kozol, 1988; McChesney, 1986; Wright & Lam, 1986). In 1978, there were 370,000 more low-cost housing units than there were low-income renters. By 1985, the situation had been dramatically reversed, and the number of low-income renters outnumbered the number of low-cost units by 3.7 million (Harrington-Lueker, 1989). Similar reversals are evident in funding patterns. The Housing and Urban

Development (HUD) low-income housing programs operated under a $33 billion budget in 1981 and a $7 billion budget in 1989. Programs to help homeless people, which were funded at less than $2 billion annually (Burns, 1991), are hardly an equitable trade-off for the $26 billion dollar loss in the housing program..

For the 32 million people living in poverty in the United States, fewer than 25,000 new, federally subsidized units of low-income housing are produced annually (Burns, 1991). The Department of Housing and Urban Development (HUD) estimates that 70,000 public housing units sit boarded up because they are too expensive to repair (Witt, 1988). In 1970, 8.5 million low-income housing units rented for less than $250. In 1987, only 6.6 million units were available for a comparable price in adjusted dollars (Mihaly, 1991). Only 6% of the rental units built in 1988 rented for less than $350 dollars. More than half the units built that year rented for $550 or more (Mihaly, 1991). Because of federal budget cuts, only 27% of poor renters receive any federal housing assistance. In many communities, families have to wait years for housing assistance. For example, there is an 8-year wait for housing assistance in the District of Columbia (Witt, 1988).

Many poor families are forced to spend a disproportionate percentage of their income for housing, leaving little money for other necessities such as food and health care. Assistance provided to families under the federal Aid to Families with Dependent Children (AFDC) program ("welfare") includes an allowance for rent. Federal funding for AFDC grants has fallen 70% since 1981 (Witt, 1988), and frequently the total AFDC payment per month does not even cover the cost of rent. When comparing AFDC grants for a family of four to the fair market rent (FMR) for housing, the problem is readily apparent. For example, the maximum AFDC grant for a family of four in Indiana is $316 per month while the FMR in Indiana is $292. In Florida, the AFDC grant size is $284 per month and the FMR is $283. In Maryland, the AFDC is $418 per month and the FMR is $376. In Texas, the FMR of $244 is greater than the AFDC grant size of $201. The average AFDC grant in 1990 was $364 for a family of three, which places the family at a level that is less than half the federal poverty standard (Mihaly, 1991).

Obvious irrationalities exist when comparing AFDC grant amounts made directly to families and the amount of money that agencies pay to sustain welfare hotels used to shelter homeless families. The city of New York pays $1,500 to $3,000 per month to house a single family in unsanitary and dangerous communal living quarters (Kozol, 1988; Kurtz, 1987). It costs the District of Columbia $90 per day to house a family of three in its welfare hotels (Rowe, 1986). Yet the federal government will supply the same family an AFDC grant of only $340 per month to cover rent and pay all other living expenses.

5

Other programs have been initiated in an attempt to help families procure affordable housing. Under Section 8 of the Public Housing Program, low-income families can receive a certificate that will provide for rental costs in excess of 30% of their income up to the FMR. Landlord participation in the program is voluntary. Of the households who receive these certificates, 52% return them, unused, because they cannot find landlords willing to participate in the program renting apartments at or below the FMR (Witt, 1988).

Family Financial Crises. During a family crisis caused by job loss, medical emergencies, fires, rent increases, or insurmountable debts, families may lose their homes (Rafferty & Rollins, 1990).

Fully two thirds of the instances of homelessness among families in the District of Columbia occur as the result of evictions (Melnick & Williams, 1987). These families may not have relatives or friends to turn to for support. Homeless families may seek refuge in temporary shelters or "welfare hotels" (Wasem, 1989a) and may be forced to rely on the charity of others. Most shelters limit stays to 7 days, forcing families to move frequently (Mihaly, 1991). Transience may be one of the most devastating aspects of homelessness (Harrington-Lueker, 1989).

"No-Fault" Divorce Laws. The increase in the number of homeless families is compounded through "no-fault" divorce laws that have been adopted in almost all of the states (Weitzman, 1985). Under these laws, the family home may be sold at the time of a divorce so that the husband and wife can split the money evenly. Prior to the enactment of the "no-fault" divorce laws, the house was typically awarded to the wife and children. It is now common for divorced women to experience a 73% drop in their standard of living (Weitzman, 1985) and be left without a home for themselves or their children, who continue to be awarded to the custody of the mother. Between 1970 and 1982, the number of children living with divorced women doubled. By 1984, 10.9 million children were being raised by single mothers (Women's Bureau, 1985).

Runaway and Throwaway Youth. A growing number of children are homeless because they have been thrown or forced out of troubled homes (Palenski & Launer, 1987). These children who run away from stressful situations have been described as "throwaways" (Stronge & Tenhouse, 1990); their plight has intensified as many resort to illegal vocations to survive on the street. Between 1 and 1.5 million youth (ages 10–17) run away from home each year (Powers, Eckenrode, & Jaklitsch, 1988). Most are victims of dysfunctional families or of failed foster care or other child welfare placements. Studies indicate that up to 75% of runaway youth are fleeing situations of severe maltreatment, including physical and sexual abuse (Farber, McCoard, Kinast, & Baum-Falkner, 1984).

Runaway and throwaway youth are at a higher risk than the average population for engaging in self-destructive behaviors; abusing substances; and having physical and mental health problems and exposure to the human immunodeficiency virus (HIV) (Powers, Eckenrode, & Jaklitsch, 1988; Witt, 1988).

The numbers of runaway and throwaway youth have increased dramatically enough that the federal government has addressed the issue in legislation. In 1974 the Runaway Youth Act, enacted as Title III of the Juvenile Justice and Delinquency Prevention Act (P.L. 98-473), provided grants and technical assistance to communities and nonprofit agencies to meet the needs of "unaccompanied" youth outside the juvenile justice system. In recognition of the fact that many runaways are actually throwaways (Sullivan & Damrosch, 1987), the 1980 reenactment of the legislation included renaming the mandate the Runaway and Homeless Youth Act (P.L. 96-509). Shelters operating under the Runaway and Homeless Youth Act report an increase in the number of youth being sheltered who have severe mental health problems. One study found that almost 50% of the adolescents living in runaway youth shelters in New York City had contemplated or attempted suicide, 30% were depressed, and 59% had school problems (Witt, 1988).

Other Factors Contributing to the Rise in Homelessness Among Children. Although not included in homeless counts, some infants are homeless at birth. These are the infants who are abandoned at the hospital and are commonly referred to as "boarder babies." Recent increases in the number of boarder babies can be correlated to increases in other areas of health concern. Mothers who carry HIV, who have AIDS, or who are the sexual partners of HIV- or AIDS-infected persons may abandon their babies at the time of delivery rather than face a challenging and potentially expensive caregiving situation. Some mothers abandon their babies in the hospital because they do not believe they have adequate resources to care for the infants. Boarder babies are homeless children who must rely on the social service system for foster care placements. Homelessness is the primary reason for foster care placement for a large number of children (Witt, 1988), and many families who are in desperate need of shelter do not request it for fear that their children will be taken away from them (Waxman & Reyes, 1987).

General Outcomes of Homelessness

Disintegration of the Family. In addition to the stress placed on families through homelessness, public assistance programs may inadvertently promote the demise of the family structure. Shelters can specify the population they serve, and three major types of shelters exist (Mihaly, 1991). The first type allows women, female children, and male children under the age of 12. The second type of shelter admits men and older boys. A third, but less commonly seen, type of shelter admits families. Such specificity may force a family to split up to acquire accommodations (Mihaly, 1991; Rosenman & Stein, 1990; Waxman & Reyes, 1987; Witt, 1988). In addition to physically separating families, shelter life may undermine traditional parenting roles. Shelter personnel may assume the responsibilities of defining bedtimes, mealtimes, menus, and other elements of daily routine (Mihaly, 1991). Shelters usually lack recreation and play areas and require that children be kept quiet and in the constant supervision of a parent. This adds pressure to the parent-child relationship (Rosenman & Stein, 1990). Parents are hindered in job searches as some shelters are emptied at 7:00 a.m. and inhabitants line up at the door to ensure a spot inside for that night (Mihaly, 1991). Studies indicate that families may voluntarily or involuntarily lose their children to a variety of other living arrangements because of shelter requirements (Hall & Maza, 1990; Mihaly, 1991).

Comparisons to Similar Socioeconomic Status Children in Homes. Children who are housed but living in abject poverty may demonstrate many of the same adverse outcomes as children who are homeless (Linehan, 1989). Studies that compare homeless children with housed children of similar socioeconomic status demonstrate that homelessness is most devastating to preschoolers, but outcomes are similar for school-aged children and youth. Of the homeless preschoolers studied, 50% demonstrate significant delays on the Denver Developmental Screening Test as compared to 16% of the housed preschoolers (Bassuk & Rosenberg, 1990).

Homeless preschoolers were less likely to be enrolled in early childhood programs such as Head Start than their housed peers and were significantly delayed in receptive vocabulary and visual-motor development (Rescoria, Parker, & Stolley, 1991). Homeless preschoolers also demonstrated significantly higher rates of behavioral and emotional symptoms (Rescoria, Parker, & Stolley, 1991). Among the school-aged population, retention, failure rates, and special education enrollment were comparable between the two groups (Bassuk & Rosenberg, 1990; Rescoria, Parker, & Stolley, 1991). Abject poverty has the greatest influence on prognosis for developmental outcomes, regardless of whether the child is housed or homeless (Mihaly, 1991). Every 5 years, the number of children who die because of poverty-related problems exceeds the number of casualties of the Vietnam War (Witt, 1988).

Effects of Homelessness on Children

Health Concerns. Although homelessness is potentially devastating for everyone, it appears to have the most detrimental effects on children and youth (Friedman & Christiansen, 1990). Serious health problems faced by homeless children include lack of food and poor nutrition (Rafferty & Rollins, 1989; Waxman & Reyes, 1987). Hunger and inadequate nutrition lead to a poor prognosis for adequate physical and cognitive development. Homeless children have more health problems than matched children of low socioeconomic status who are living at home. A study of the health status of 158 homeless children living in Washington, DC documented the existence of four times more health problems than are found in the general pediatric population in the United States (Miller & Linn, 1988).

Like many families in poverty, homeless families typically do not seek health services for their children until the child's health forces them to do so. Even then, many homeless parents are unable to maintain a medical regimen prescribed by a physician because of their living conditions (Wright, 1990). Sixty-five percent of homeless children have one or more acute or chronic health problems, and newborns are at the highest risk for experiencing severe health problems (Bass, Brennan, Mehta, & Kodzis, 1990).

Homeless youth demonstrate twice the rate of chronic disease as is found in the housed population (Wright, 1990). The most common chronic illnesses in homeless children and youth include eye disorders, ear problems, gastrointestinal disorders, neurologic impairments, dental problems, and genito-urinary dysfunctions (Wright, 1990).

In comparison to children of low socioeconomic status who are living at home, homeless children are three times more likely to exhibit elevated lead levels (Alperstein, Rappaport, & Flanigan, 1988). Research indicates that elevated lead levels may produce neurologic functioning deficits, leading to serious educational problems. Analyses demonstrate that neither demographics nor substance abuse characteristics are the major factors leading to chronic illness. The major factor for the illnesses is the homelessness itself (Wright, 1990).

Psychological Concerns. Homeless children demonstrate a variety of social and psychological traits attributable to their homelessness (Rafferty & Rollins, 1989). Homeless children's reactions to their situations depend in large part upon their age, gender, and temperament; the length of time they have been homeless; the cause of their homelessness; and the existence of support systems (Linehan, 1989). Small studies have documented specific psychological reactions to homelessness. Expected reactions to becoming homeless include aggression and noncompliance or shyness and withdrawal (Bassuk & Gallagher, 1990; Mihaly, 1991). Homeless children may exhibit extreme stress reactions and poor self-esteem (Stronge & Tenhouse, 1990; Waxman & Reyes, 1987). Of the children older than 18 months, 70% exhibit mood problems, and 40%

have difficulty interacting with other children and adults (Layzer, Goodson, & deLange, 1986).

Homeless children and youth are more susceptible to depression than are their peers with homes (Linehan, 1989), and almost 50% of the homeless preschool population is clinically depressed (Children's Defense Fund, 1988). Anywhere from 31% to 50% of the population of homeless children and youth may need referral for psychiatric evaluation (Bassuk & Rosenberg, 1988; Bassuk & Rubin, 1987), and the majority indicate experiencing suicidal thoughts. The homeless population scores equal to or higher than the mean demonstrated by children and youth who are emotionally disturbed in the areas of sleep problems, aggression, shyness, and withdrawal (Bassuk & Gallagher, 1990).

Abuse and Neglect. It is not uncommon for children to find themselves homeless as a result of domestic violence (Martin, 1976). Over 70% of the children brought to shelters for battered women by their mothers have also been abused (Layzer, Goodson, & deLange, 1986). As might be expected, these children display problems with health, psychosocial development, and relationships (Martin, 1976).

Intellectual Development. Poor prenatal and postnatal care increases the chance that a child will demonstrate diminished capacity for cognitive and adaptive functioning (Rafferty & Rollins, 1989). The Children's Defense Fund (1988) reported that almost half of the homeless children under age 5 displayed significant developmental delays. A study conducted by Bassuk and Rubin (1987), which included 156 children in 19 shelters in and around Boston, Massachusetts, indicated high percentages of children in need of intervention to ameliorate developmental delays. Figure 1 depicts the percentages of children demonstrating multiple delays, more than four delays and deficiencies in personal/emotional, gross motor, and fine motor skills.

In a comparison of homeless and housed families of similar socioeconomic status, 54% of the homeless and 16% of the housed preschoolers demonstrated at least one major developmental delay (Bassuk & Rosenberg, 1988).

Behavioral Characteristics. Homeless children display behavioral characteristics that reflect inadequacies in their physical and mental health as well as in intellectual development. Many behaviors may be learned as necessary for survival and may indicate the child's attempts to cope with environmental situations. Often these attempts at coping are interpreted by others as inappropriate behavioral responses and are referred to as behavioral disorders (Stronge & Tenhouse, 1990). Homeless children are described as displaying more acting-out, restless, and aggressive behaviors than their peers who have homes (Linehan, 1989). Homeless

FIGURE 1
Significant Developmental Delay

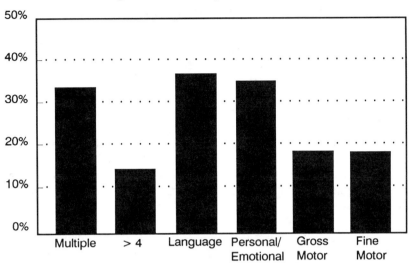

children may experience a higher incidence of sleeping problems, withdrawal, and regression behaviors (Bassuk & Rubin, 1987; Linehan, 1989). Homeless children and youth may appear to be constantly tired and anxious (Linehan, 1989).

Although major political and social changes are necessary before homelessness is substantially diminished, educational systems hold a key to providing homeless children and youth the skills necessary to create productive and stable futures. Education permits children to acquire skills needed to compete equitably in the job market (Friedman & Christiansen, 1990).

In the past, obtaining and maintaining school enrollment has been difficult for homeless children and youth. Although not completely successful, new federal initiatives encourage school systems to provide educational opportunities to homeless children and youth to the same degree afforded housed children and youth. Chapter 3 provides an overview of the federal incentives and implications for school systems.

3. Implications for Practitioners

Federal incentives have encouraged school districts to enroll homeless children and youth and maintain their school attendance. Administrators and teachers have a variety of strategies available to them to provide equal educational opportunities to homeless students.

Federal Incentives

Until 1987, most legislation purporting to address the needs of the homeless population was directed at adults who were considered to be in a temporary crisis (Wasem, 1989b). The major program enacted was the Emergency Food and Shelter Program (P.L. 98-8), funded through the Federal Emergency Management Agency (FEMA). Laws were enacted (P.L. 99-198 and P.L. 99-570) that enhanced the ability of a person without a fixed mailing address to obtain access to existing federal programs such as AFDC, Medicaid, and Supplemental Security Incom (SSI). The first piece of legislation to recognize the implications of homelessness for education is the Stewart B. McKinney Homeless Assistance Act (P.L. 100-77).

Stewart B. McKinney Act. The Stewart B. McKinney Homeless Assistance Act (P.L. 100-77), passed in 1987, was the first comprehensive support program for America's homeless population. The programs authorized by the McKinney Act include primary health care, emergency food and shelter, mental health and substance abuse services, transitional housing, social services, education, and job training.

One program in the Act contains policies and procedures for ensuring that homeless children receive an appropriate education. The education portion of the law, Subtitle VII-B, is administered by the U. S. Department of Education. This subtitle guarantees children and youth who are homeless the same access to elementary and secondary education as children who are not homeless. The 1987 Act required that states address and revise residency, guardianship, or other enrollment criteria that prevent homeless students from attending school. State education agencies were encouraged to voluntarily submit applications for federal grants. The 1987 Act delineated that grant money be used to

1. Secure a coordinator for the education of homeless children and youth, who, among other activities, must identify special educational needs of the homeless population.

2. Compile data on the number of children who are homeless within their state and document the problems these children encounter in gaining school access.

3. Develop a state plan for educating students who are homeless, which should include guarantees of enrollment based on the student's best interest; dispute-resolution strategies; assurances of the extension of special services such as compensatory education programs, education programs for children with disabilities, services for gifted and talented students, programs for students whose native language is not English, vocational education programs, and school meal programs; and mechanisms for the timely transfer of school records when a student moves from one district to another.

During the first year of implementation, all 50 states and the District of Columbia applied for McKinney grants (Jackson, 1989). The grants were allocated according to a population-based formula, and each state received at least $50,000. During the second year of implementation, 49 states, the District of Columbia, and Puerto Rico submitted state plans and applied for grants. The state of Hawaii was the only state that chose not to participate (Jackson, 1989).

Three years after the passage of the McKinney Act, national reports estimated that a significant number of school-aged children who were homeless were still not attending school regularly. With this in mind, the Stewart B. McKinney Homeless Assistance Amendments Act of 1990 (P.L. 101-645) was passed. The 1987 Act required states to remove residency-related policies that were interfering with school attendance of children and youth who were homeless. The 1990 Amendments recognize that residency requirements have not uniformly been resolved and that school and immunization record transfer, transportation, and guardianship requirements continue to prevent the enrollment and retention of homeless children and youth. The 1990 Amendments contain provisions for the coordination, development, and delivery of educational services to children and youth who are homeless.

Title V of the 1990 Amendments authorizes $6 million for fiscal year (FY) 1991, $7.5 million for FY 1992, and such sums as may be necessary for FY 1993 for the coordination of education for the homeless population. The Department of Education may make grants to states to maintain an Office of the Coordinator of the Education of Homeless Children and Youth. The activities of the state coordinator have been expanded to include the coordination and provision of comprehensive services to homeless children and youth; the development and implementation of parent, professional, and service provider education regarding the rights and needs of homeless children and youth; and the development and instigation of strategies to ensure that homeless children and youth receive the services for which they are eligible, including federal, state, or local nutrition and before- and after-school care programs. The 1990 Amendments change the reporting responsibilities of the state coordinator from once a year to once every 2 years.

The 1990 Amendments authorize funding for the development of exemplary programs for homeless children and youth. Title V provides for $4 million for FY 1991, $5 million for FY 1992, and such sums as may be necessary for FY 1993 for grants to state and local education agencies that have demonstrated excellence in removing the barriers that interfere with school enrollment and retention of homeless children and youth.

Title V authorizes $25 million for FY 1991 and such sums as may be necessary for FYs 1992 and 1993 for grants to state and local education agencies for providing educational services to homeless children and youth. The 1990 Amendments stipulate that at least 50% of the funding be used for tutoring, remedial education services, or other educational services to homeless children and youth. At least 35%, but not more than 50%, may be used to provide necessary support services, including transportation, referrals to health care services, fees for records transfer, and the provision of before- and after-school care and summer programs.

The 1990 Amendments clarify that students who become homeless during the summer must be allowed to remain at their previous academic year school for the following academic year. The 1990 Amendments also state the insufficiency of homelessness, by itself, as a reason for separation of students from the mainstream environment. State and local education agencies should develop and adopt policies that ensure that homeless children and youth are not isolated or stigmatized.

For FY 1991, $680 million was appropriated for the programs outlined in the McKinney Act as compared to $355 million in FY 1987. Most of the monies are directed toward state and local governments and nonprofit agencies to fund supportive housing, health care, education, community services, emergency food and shelter services, and family support (Mihaly, 1991). The McKinney Act does not address the need for basic income support or affordable housing.

Although the McKinney Act and subsequent amendments have had a considerable impact on the awareness of the need to ensure educational services to children who are homeless, the victory is tenuous at best. In comparison to other federal legislation that has shaped educational programming, the McKinney Act stands as an idealistic but weak advocate for services (Stronge & Helm, 1990). All that a state or territory must do to secure federal funding is submit a credible plan. In dramatic contrast to the Individuals with Disabilities Education Act (IDEA) (P.L. 101-476, reenactment of the Education for All Handicapped Children Act, P.L. 94-142), participation in McKinney Act programs is voluntary and there are no consequences for noncompliance (Bowen, Purrington, Layton, & O'Brien, 1989; Rafferty & Rollins, 1990). Barriers to school enrollment and retention persist, and the Department of Education has been ineffective in implementing comprehensive change (Friedman & Christiansen, 1990), leaving state and local education agencies to shoulder the responsibility for change (Stronge & Helm, 1990). The National Law Center on Homelessness and Poverty conducted a 20-state survey of providers of services to the homeless in 1989 and found that 60% reported the continued use of residency requirements to exclude homeless children from school. Forty percent documented the use of guardianship requirements for the same purpose. Fifty-five percent reported that homeless children and youth were not being afforded services comparable to those given to housed children, including the extension of school meals and special education services (Friedman & Christiansen, 1990). Concerted effort needs to be directed toward accomplishing the intent of the McKinney Act.

Runaway and Homeless Youth Program (RHYP). In addition to the McKinney Act (P.L. 100-628), the Runaway and Homeless Youth Program (RHYP) attempts to meet the needs of the homeless children and youth. The Runaway Youth Act was enacted as Title III, part D, section 341, of the Juvenile Justice and Delinquency Prevention Act (P.L. 98-473). In 1980, the Act was expanded to address issues related to homeless youth in general and was renamed the Runaway and Homeless Youth Act (RHYA), in recognition of the increasing numbers of youth who were being forced out of home environments. The Runaway and Homeless Youth Program (RHYP) is administered by the Department of Health and Human Services and is authorized to provide shelters, coordinated networks, community-based centers, and demonstration programs for runaway and homeless youth and their families. The RHYP funds the National Runaway Switchboard, which links callers with community resources, families, and counselors. The RHYP also operates an Adolescent Suicide Hotline (Witt, 1988). The RHYP has been reauthorized as part of the Omnibus Drug Initiative (P.L. 100-690). More than 300 shelters are assisted by the RHYP. These shelters typically enforce a maximum stay of 15 days (Mihaly, 1991). In a 1988 amendment to the Runaway and Homeless Youth Act, Congress made funding available for grants to establish transitional and independent living programs. In addition, a nonprofit organization, the National Network of Runaway and Youth Services, has over 1,000 community-based agencies that serve homeless and runaway youth.

Educational Implications

The combination of physical, psychological, intellectual, and behavioral outcomes of homelessness for children and youth may make it difficult for them to achieve in school. Homelessness has been described as a "breeding ground" for disabling conditions (Russell & Williams, 1988). Homeless children and youth who manage to attend school may exhibit unsatisfactory school progress. Children and youth who are homeless are at risk for a variety of school-related learning problems (Bass et al., 1990; Eddowes & Hranitz, 1989; Linehan, 1989). Research indicates that students who are homeless have greater difficulty in making transitions, being successful with academic tasks, interacting positively with peers, and demonstrating a healthy self-concept (Stronge & Tenhouse, 1990).

A study conducted in Boston demonstrated that 40% of the students who were homeless were failing or performing below-average work, 25% were in special classes, and 43% had repeated one grade (Bassuk & Rubin, 1987). Of the homeless students who could be tracked for 2 years, 56% averaged two to six school transfers and had higher rates of grade repetition (Rafferty & Rollins, 1989). Homeless children are also more likely to develop behavior problems than their peers (Bassuk & Rosenberg, 1988; Russell & Williams, 1988). Homeless children and youth may demonstrate an increased need for special service provision (Friedman & Christiansen, 1990).

Although they are clearly at risk for academic failure, the transient nature of most homeless students makes the time-consuming task of assessment and referral for special services almost impossible. Given the high percentages of homeless students experiencing school problems, child counts in special education should reflect service provision to a considerable number of learners with exceptionalities who are homeless (Rivlin, 1986). Analyses not only fail to document the existence of homelessness among students in special education, they also demonstrate that homeless students are often denied access to any educational opportunities. Educational access depends on the alteration of administrative policies that exclude homeless students from school enrollment and attendance.

Implications for Administrators

Administrators are charged not only to increase their awareness of the plight of children and youth who are homeless, but also to develop strategies for meeting the students' educational needs. The biggest challenge facing administrators involves the circumvention of the barriers that inhibit uninterrupted school attendance by students who are homeless.

Unfortunately, educational intervention has proven to be elusive for many homeless children and youth. It is estimated that between 28% (Cavazos, 1990) and 43% (Ely, 1987) of homeless school-aged children do not attend school. A median estimate of these percentages would indicate that 67,000 homeless children do not attend school (Bowen, et al., 1989). A variety of legal, financial, bureaucratic, social, and familial

FIGURE 2
Barriers That Exclude Homeless Children and
Youth from Educational Services

Transportation Issues
- Cost
- Time
- Convenience

Social Barriers
- Transience
- Potential problems with social acceptance
- High drop-out rate

Legal Barriers
- Residency Requirements
- Guardianship Requirements

Financial Constraints
- Prioritize meeting of basic needs
- Lack of clothing and/or school supplies
- Reluctance of community to commit finances

Bureaucratic Barriers
- Transfer of records
- Time required to refer, assess, and place in appropriate special education programs
- Inability to track students for coordinated efforts
- Lack of support services

Familial Barriers
- Need to focus on survival priorities
- Fear of discovery
- Sibling care
- Wage earning

barriers serve to effectively exclude homeless children and youth from accessing educational opportunities (Bowen, et al., 1989; Cavazos, 1990; Eddowes & Hranitz, 1989; Ely, 1987; Jackson, 1989; Rafferty & Rollins, 1989; Rosenman & Stein, 1990; Schumack, 1987; Stronge & Tenhouse, 1990). These interrelated barriers, presented in Figure 2, effectively deny many homeless children and youth access to a free, appropriate public education.

Transportation Issues. State agencies indicate that poor transportation (lacking or inconvenient) is the major reason that homeless children are unable to access educational opportunities (Cavazos, 1990). The cost of transportation varies according to student location, which may change frequently. The amount of time that must be devoted to being transported can also become prohibitive as students move. The use of community transportation resources may present tremendous challenges related to convenience. If a school is willing to allow a student to continue attending after a residence change, the student may be faced with using public transportation systems that could include multiple line changes and connections. Access to the school's transportation system may involve getting to a pick-up point that is a considerable distance from the new shelter or residence. Students must also obtain enough money to access the transportation system. Without provisions for transportation, the promise of maintaining consistent educational placement is unrealistic (Jackson, 1989).

Social Barriers. Transience may present the greatest barrier to school attendance. As many as 80% of sheltered homeless students are not from the local area (Hall & Maza, 1990). Being constantly on the move, students are unable to establish any familiarity with a school, its personnel, or its students. Likewise, the school community may not have time to accept the new student before the student's residence changes again.

Like other students, homeless children may be concerned about their appearance and acceptance by classmates. Homeless children and youth may be reluctant to attend school because they lack the appropriate clothing and/or school supplies. A lack of time for the affiliation process to occur and perceived inferiorities from the homeless student's perspective as well as the school system's perspective may make social acceptance difficult. Homeless students report being referred to as "shelter kids" (Rosenman & Stein, 1990) and experiencing ostracism because of their homelessness (Hall & Maza, 1990; Waxman & Reyes, 1987). Due to a higher than typical incidence of behavior problems, students who are homeless may not be accepted by the school community.

Research indicates that peers as well as teachers may avoid interacting with students with behavior problems. A lack of social acceptance coupled with potential academic difficulties creates a situation that does not encourage homeless students to persevere in their efforts to maintain school attendance. Consequently, dropout rates are higher among students who are homeless.

Legal Barriers. Specific enrollment criteria such as residency requirements and guardianship issues act as legal barriers to educational
opportunities. Traditionally, schools will serve only those students who
reside within district lines. The transient nature of homelessness may
cause a student to move into and out of a specific district several times
within a school year. Typical school expectations also mandate that
enrollment in a particular school is dependent on the residence of the
student's guardian. Living arrangements for homeless students may
vacillate between a variety of relatives and friends, none of whom are
legal guardians. So although a student may live in a certain district, the
district may be unwilling to provide educational opportunities because
the student's legal guardian resides in another district. Although the
1987 McKinney Act made these practices illegal, 60% of the states sur-
veyed still use residency as justification for exclusion (Mihaly, 1991).

Bureaucratic Barriers. Schools require the presentation of specific records
before a student may be enrolled. Generally, a parent or guardian must
present previous school records and documentation of medical history,
including inoculation records. Frequently, students who are homeless
do not possess this documentation, and school districts will deny the
student's right to attend school. In some cases, districts will attempt to
transfer a student's records from one school to another. Records transfer
is typically inefficient and slow. Most public school systems have not yet
developed coordinated and effective methods of transferring records and
tracking students during residence changes. Such efforts are usually the
parents' responsibility; parents who are homeless may lack the time and
resources to accomplish transferring tasks.

Research on the cognitive and psychological development of children and youth who are homeless has demonstrated that specialized or
remedial interventions may be necessary before academic success will be
realized. In the public education system, specialized services are provided only after the student has been properly referred, assessed, and
deemed eligible by an educational decision-making committee. The
entire process could legally take as long as 3 months. The transience
associated with being homeless does not allow for resolution of the time
issues related to bureaucratic guidelines for provision of special services.
Students who are homeless are usually not in one place long enough to
be found eligible for special education services and consequently do not
receive specialized support services.

Financial Constraints. Although the public school system in this country
is considered to be "free," certain items that facilitate school achievement
and acceptance must be purchased. Students who are homeless may not
have the necessary financial resources available. For example, students
are told which school supplies to bring and can enhance peer and adult

acceptance by wearing certain clothes. There are usually some costs associated with field trips and extracurricular activities. Although education is provided free of charge, adult and peer acceptance, the ability to produce products, and access to enhancement activities are dependent on adequate resources. Students who are homeless may be limited by financial constraints.

School districts may attempt to implement programs to defray some of the costs of becoming a participating member of a school community. Unfortunately, school districts rely on community sources of finance, and communities may be unwilling to commit funds to subsidize the education of homeless students. Although the practice is being challenged, school districts usually receive funding according to the tax base of the community. Communities may take a dim view of committing finances to a population of students who may not reside in the district and whose parents or guardians may not be taxpayers.

Familial Factors. School attendance is also influenced by familial factors (Cavazos, 1990). School enrollment may be a lower priority for parents who are struggling to provide the basic needs of food, shelter, and clothing for their children. School enrollment may be undesirable if the family is in hiding from potential or actual threats. Parents may also want older children to care for younger siblings or secure jobs during the day to earn money, products, or services.

One of the most efficient methods of enabling a student to overcome the detrimental effects of homelessness is to provide an appropriate education. Unfortunately, some of the legal provisions designed to extend appropriate education to children with disabilities can actually present formidable barriers that deny access to educational opportunities. Although IDEA guarantees all students the right to a free, appropriate public education, the lengthy referral and eligibility determination process has served to deny special service provisions. To overcome the barriers encountered in attempting to gain access to the regular education system, as well as to secure special services as needed, the federal government has initiated legislative incentives so that children and youth who are homeless may receive access to the education system. Once inside the system, homeless children and youth will be best served by teachers who are aware of the educational needs created by homelessness.

Implications for Teachers

Children with Special Needs. Homelessness may create a situation in which developmental delays will be demonstrated (Russell & Williams, 1988). From conception, children who are born into homelessness are at risk for such delays. Homelessness results in poor prenatal care, poor maternal nutrition, and poor birth outcomes, which are generally not compensated for by the postnatal environment. One study demonstrated that almost 11% of the population of homeless children have disabilities, with learning disabilities being the most common, followed by speech impairments, mental retardation, and emotional disturbance (Russell & Williams, 1988). It is predicted that emotional disturbance becomes the most commonly applied diagnosis the longer the children remain homeless (Russell & Williams, 1988), as the children develop coping behaviors that may not be acceptable to the school system. IDEA guarantees a free, appropriate public education to all school-age children and youth, including those with disabilities. The McKinney Act serves to encourage the abolishment of legal and bureaucratic barriers to the extension of educational opportunities. Taken together, the two pieces of legislation promote the provision of special services to homeless students who are deemed eligible. Unfortunately, homeless children may not be enrolled in one school long enough for eligibility to be determined. In addition, tougher academic standards resulting from the "excellence" movement selectively exclude most homeless children and have severe ramifications for students with special needs (Kozol, 1990).

General Teaching Strategies. An increasing awareness and knowledge of how children are affected by homelessness can help school personnel implement strategies to support students' efforts and alleviate anxieties and stress (Linehan, 1989). School personnel must learn to plan for and incorporate homeless students into their programs for whatever period of time the children will be able to attend (Eddowes & Hranitz, 1989; Schumack, 1987). They must also make concerted efforts to retain students despite transience (Gewirtzman & Fodor, 1987). Toward these ends, the U.S. Department of Education lists the following as the top six priorities for meeting the special educational needs of children and youth who are homeless (Cavazos, 1990):

- Remediation and tutoring of basic skills.
- Support services including counseling and social work services.
- After-school and/or extended-day services to provide basic needs and recreation.
- Awareness training for personnel.
- Educational assessment, screening, and placement.
- Program continuity and stability.

In addition to the needs prioritized by Cavazos (1990), Buffa (1990) and Waxman and Reyes (1987) have made the following recommendations for meeting the educational needs of students who are homeless:

- Establish definite lines of communication between and among service agencies and schools.
- Conduct joint training to facilitate networking.
- Develop outreach programs that include the creation of resource guides for parents and teachers.
- Develop shelter-based tutoring and educational assistance.

Teachers can assist students who are homeless through consideration of a few critical components: personal space, identity development, and the establishment of a structured environment.

Homeless children and youth typically fail to develop a sense of personal space and personal place. *Personal space* was defined by Rivlin (1990) as being the protective distance an individual maintains between self and others. *Personal places* are specific areas that "belong" to a person (e.g., spot at the dinner table, room, bed) (Rivlin, 1990). School programs can enable students who are homeless to develop the concepts of personal space and personal place by defining spaces in the school building that are the student's own and by marking the spaces with symbols of the student's identity. These simple efforts will help the student to develop a sense of self-worth and stability (Rivlin, 1990).

Homeless children may become distrustful of adults for failing to provide shelter, food, and protection. In addition, homeless children may be forced to assume adult roles at an early age (Bassuk & Gallagher, 1990). Schools need to provide a safe environment where the child can be a child and explore his or her own personal characteristics. Schools need to concentrate efforts on getting homeless students into programs and keeping them there. Basic needs must take precedence as schools focus on providing transportation, food, and support for emotional development (Bassuk & Gallagher, 1990). Teachers should make sure that parents/caregivers are aware of support programs available through the schools (e.g., free lunch and breakfast). The availability of support programs should be communicated discreetly to avoid embarrassment or defensive reactions. It is critical that the teacher take the initiative to follow up on the suggestions in case the parent has misplaced contact information or has met with resistance from service agencies.

Homelessness and missed educational opportunities may confound the student's ability to acquire certain skills, including social and emotional competence. Teachers must not assume that any student knows what to do, but should informally assess the student's abilities and develop appropriate interventions. Skill acquisition will be facilitated if the task is broken into small steps and multimodal methods of presentation are used. The assignment of achievable class roles will foster a sense of control and responsibility.

Teachers will be better able to meet the educational needs of students who are homeless if they are allowed to be autonomous and nurturing and to focus on strengthening a positive parent-child interaction (Neiman, 1988). A structured, stable, nonthreatening environment will enable students who are homeless to express their feelings and will foster a positive sense of self-worth (Gewirtzman & Fodor, 1987). Teachers can emphasize student success and tell students about extracurricular opportunities that may enhance their feelings of self-worth.

Students who are homeless need more than access to education; they need a high-quality education tailored to compensate for negative life stressors (Kayne, 1989). A study conducted by Rescoria, Parker, and Stolley (1991) clearly demonstrates the importance of school attendance. In this study, the researchers found that the outcomes for homeless school-aged children were similar to the outcomes for housed children of similar socioeconomic status if the homeless children were attending school.

4. Implications for Program Development and Administration

Networking is the essential component for developing effective educational services for homeless children and youth.

Providing effective services to homeless children and their families is extremely complex. The problems facing these families are compounded because they cross the spectrum of all disciplines. Unfortunately, most services, staff, and resources are overextended, resulting in services to homeless children and their families that are limited, isolated, poorly coordinated, and ineffective in addressing the needs of this population.

Management tools can help address the complex issue of homelessness. *Networking* is an effective management tool in addressing issues and services that cross multidisciplinary areas by focusing on a specific issue—homeless children. By combining network resources and efforts, outcomes can be maximized. Issues such as education, health care, mental health, housing, and alcohol and other drug abuse can be effectively addressed through a multidisciplinary approach that promotes coordination, communication, and collaboration.

Two important groundrules are critical for effective networking:

1. Turf issues must be set aside by network members in order to provide a full array of services to homeless and runaway children, youth, and their families.

2. Networking should be proactive rather than reactive in seeking funds to meet the needs of runaway and homeless children and youth.

Networking brings together people with a shared responsibility to address an identified issue. People tend to work harder for a cause when they and their clients benefit from collaborative actions. Often there is no natural or spontaneous grouping of people around a single purpose. A strategy needs to be developed to bring organizations, agencies, and individuals together to determine whether or not a vehicle to promote communication and collaboration such as a network is a feasible solution.

When exploring the development of a network, it is important to define clearly the major issue or objective of the network. The major issue or objective must be simply stated so that it can be communicated clearly to potential network participants.

After developing a clear, concise statement of the major issue or objective of the potential network, two lists need to be compiled. The first list is a computation of possible network members to ensure a multidisciplinary approach, including leaders from all systems that impact on the major issues or objectives and the community at large. Being inclusive rather than exclusive in membership development removes the perception of elitism, which can undermine the entire networking concept. Potential members of the network will remove themselves from participation in the network for various reasons, leaving a strong base of interested participants.

A second list should contain possible conveners of the network. Possible conveners are organizations, agencies, or individuals who provide leadership in targeted systems or communities. Four important characteristics should be considered when compiling the list of possible conveners and determining the convener of the proposed network:

1. *Neutrality*—ability to be nonpartisan; a body that will not benefit directly by convening the network and has no specific issue to promote; a neutral body such as a college, university, community planning group, or community leader (e.g., university faculty, bank president, church leader) are ideal possibilities; a body providing direct service related to the major objective or issue should not be given high priority.

2. *Commitment*—shared value, belief, and importance of the major objective or issue identified.

3. *Facilitation*—ability to facilitate, promote, and support the organizational process of the network development.

4. *Recognition*—ability and power to convene key leaders.

After the outlined activities are completed, a wealth of information will be available to guide the selection of the network convener and potential members of the network. Preliminary meetings will be necessary to allow potential members to determine the feasibility of developing a network and the molding of its organizational structure.

Combining limited resources to maximize outcomes is a key result of successful networking. When faced with an overwhelming and difficult task, networking provides the following benefits:

- Reduces burnout.
- Avoids overload on one specific system and/or resource (staff, funds, etc.).
- Increases referral and resource bases for members.
- Provides peer support.
- Increases understanding from the perspective of different disciplines.
- Stimulates planning and program development.
- Provides an advocacy voice.
- Provides a legislative voice.
- Enhances communication.
- Increases interagency linkages.
- Increases joint proposal writing.
- Increases an agency's opportunities to promote a specialized area of expertise to other network members which can increase the agency's funding base.
- Increases the availability of high-quality, low-cost training.
- Sets standards.

An Exemplary Program

When systems are faced with increasingly complex issues and decreasing resources, networking vehicles such as the Runaway and Homeless

FIGURE 3
Runaway and Homeless Youth Network of Allegheny Country

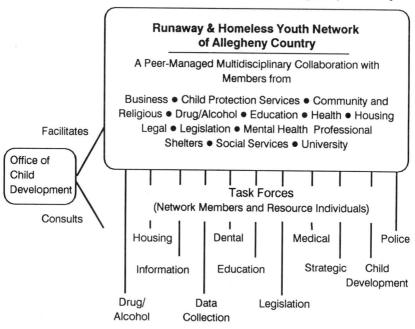

Youth Network of Allegheny County are innovative management tools to increase the availability and quality of services. This model can be replicated in rural, suburban, or urban areas. The networking model provides organizational flexibility and a structure that can be molded to meet the needs of the participants. The network structure can include committees, task forces, and interest groups as subsets of the main networking body.

The Runaway and Homeless Youth Network of Allegheny County meets monthly to provide network communication and coordination. As interests in specific areas are identified, an effective task force system is developed by the Network. The activities of the Network are carried out by 10 active task forces: Education, Medical, Legislation, Housing, Dental, Child Development, Information, Drug and Alcohol, Data, Police Law Enforcement, and Strategical Planning. Figure 3 depicts the organizational hierarchy of the Network.

The task forces are chaired by members at the monthly Network meeting. A unique feature of the task force system is its membership. Individuals with expertise in the specific area of the task force have the choice of participating in task force activities but may choose not to attend Network monthly meetings. The key to the high-level activity of the Network has been flexibility to adapt to the availability of its members' interests and time.

Through the efforts of the Network, over $276,000 has been specifically targeted for services to runaway and homeless children and youth in Allegheny County. In addition, over a 3-year period, network staff members have been trained through the joint collaborative network efforts in the following areas: educational issues of homeless children; AIDS; recognition of child abuse, satanism, and high-risk adolescents; dental needs of homeless children and youth; and cultural sensitivity.

Through Network collaborative efforts, two computerized county systems are being developed to collect data on runaway and homeless youth. One system will involve 43 school districts tracking homeless children through the educational system. The second computerized system will aid service providers in determining appropriate intervention and referral services to runaway and homeless youth as well as providing an agency and county database on runaway and homeless youth. Over 3,000 runaway and homeless youth information packets have been developed and distributed to legislators, policymakers, and community organizations and agencies. Most important, the Network has developed an effective system of communication and collaboration among its members.

All systems strive to produce benefits that have impact and are effective. Networking is a creative management tool that can be molded to meet the needs of group participants by providing flexible organization and structure to achieve these outcomes. Based on common belief and shared values such as the importance of education for homeless children, networking can increase the availability and quality of education and other services and affect the future lives of these children and youth by increasing their opportunities to break the cycle of poverty.

Conclusion

After a moderate amount of attention, the national attitude toward homelessness is becoming one of unavoidable acceptance. At least 100,000 children go to sleep homeless every night (Mihaly, 1991). Homelessness is often thought of as being synonymous with hopelessness, but this need not be the case. An appropriate education can help children and youth who are homeless to acquire skills that will enable them to overcome the potentially cyclic and devastating effects of a homeless situation. A variety of support services must be provided in order for the cycle to be interrupted. An appropriate education is the most promising intervention available. As directed by federal precedents and the continuous work of advocates, schools must increase their efforts to meet the needs of homeless students, including those who need special services to benefit from their educational opportunities. Realistically, schools must recognize that homeless children and youth bring with them a variety of problems. Emotional stress, behavioral disorders, physical anomalies, poor health, and developmental delays created by a transient life style, as well as cognitive deficits because of missed schooling, inhibit the ability to learn. These problems, coupled with high absenteeism and school access barriers, may deter efforts by educational personnel. Encouraged by federal mandates, school systems must increase their efforts to incorporate children and youth who are homeless into their programs. Without such efforts, homeless children will not learn the critical skills needed to gain control of their futures.

References

Alperstein, G., Rappaport, C., & Flanigan, J. (1988). Health problems of homeless children in New York City. *American Journal of Public Health, 78*(9), 1232–1233.

Bass, J. L., Brennan, P., Mehta, K. A., & Kodzis, S. (1990). Pediatric problems in a suburban shelter for homeless families. *Pediatrics, 85*(1), 33–38.

Bassuk, E. L., & Gallagher, E.M. (1990). The impact of homelessness on children. In N. A. Boxill (Ed.), *Homeless children: The watchers and the waiters* (pp. 19–33). Binghamton, NY: Haworth.

Bassuk, F., & Rosenberg, L. (1988). Why does family homelessness occur? *American Journal of Public Health, 78*, 783–88.

Bassuk, F., & Rosenberg, L. (1990). Psychosocial characteristics of homeless children and children with homes. *Pediatrics, 85*, 257–261.

Bassuk, F., & Rubin, L. (1987). Homeless children: A neglected population. *American Journal of Orthopsychiatry, 57*(2), 279–286.

Baxter, E., & Hopper, K. (1981). *Private lives/public spaces: Homeless adults on the streets of New York City.* New York: Institute for Social Welfare Research, Community Service Society.

Bowen, J. M., Purrington, G. S., Layton, D. H., & O'Brien, K. (1989, March). *Educating homeless children and youth: A policy analysis.* Paper presented at the Annual Meeting of the American Educational Research Association, San Francisco, CA.

Buffa, J. A. (1990). *Information and recommendations on homeless children for special education personnel.* Washington, DC: National Association of State Directors of Special Education.

Burns, S. (Ed.). (1991). Homelessness demographics, causes and trends. *Homewords, 3*(4), 1–3.

Cavazos, L. F. (1990, March). *U.S. Department of Education Report to Congress on the Education for Homeless Children and Youth Program for the period October 1, 1988 through September 30, 1989.*

Children's Defense Fund. (1988). *What every American should be asking political leaders in 1988: About children and the future, about leadership and vision, about national values and priorities.* Washington, DC: Author.

Eddowes, A., & Hranitz, J. R. (1989). Educating children of the homeless. *Childhood Education: Infancy through Early Adolescence, 65*(4), 197–200.

Ely, L. (1987). *Broken lives: Denial of education to homeless children.* Washington, DC: National Coalition for the Homeless.

Farber, E., McCoard, D., Kinast, C., & Baum–Falkner, D. (1984). Violence in families of adolescent runaways. *Child Abuse and Neglect, 2*(3), 173–192.

Friedman, L., & Christiansen, G. (1990). *Shut out: Denial of education to homeless children.* Washington, DC: National Law Center on Homelessness and Poverty. (ERIC Document Reproduction Service No. ED 320 987)

Gewirtzman, R., & Fodor, I. (1987). The homeless child at school: From welfare hotel to classroom. *Child Welfare, 66*(3), 237–245.

Hall, J. A. & Maza, P. L. (1990). No fixed address: The effects of homelessness on families and children. In N. A. Boxill (Ed.), *Homeless children: The watchers and the waiters* (pp. 35–47). Binghamton, NY: Haworth.

Harrington–Lueker, D. (1989). What kind of school board member would help homeless children? *American School Board Journal, 176*(7), 12–19.

Hope, M., & Young, J. (1986). *The faces of homelessness.* Lexington, MA: Lexington.

Jackson, S. (1989). *The education rights of homeless children.* Cambridge, MA: Center for Law and Education.

Kayne, A. (1989). *Annotated bibliography of social science literature concerning the education of homeless children.* Cambridge, MA: Center for Law and Education.

Kozol, J. (1988). *Rachel and her children: Homeless families in America.* New York: Crown.

Kozol, J. (1990). The new untouchables. *Newsweek Special Issue, 114*(27), 48–53.

Kurtz, H. (1987, September 15). Welfare hotel occupants at eye of political storm in New York. *The Washington Post*, p. A3.

Layzer, J. I., Goodson, B. D. & deLange, C. (1986). Children in shelters. *Children Today, 15*, 6–11.

Linehan, M. F. (1989). Homeless children: Educational strategies for school personnel. *PRISE Reporter, 21*(2), 1–2, insert.

Martin, D. (1976). *Battered wives.* New York: Simon & Schuster.

Maza, P. L., & Hall, J. A. (1988). *Homeless children and their families: A preliminary study.* Washington, DC: Child Welfare League of America.

McChesney, K. Y. (1986). Families: The new homeless. *Family Professional, 1*(1), 13–14.

Melnick, V. L. & Williams, C. S. (1987, May). *Children and families without homes: Observations from thirty case studies.* Washington, DC: University of the District of Columbia, Center for Applied Research and Urban Policy.

Mihaly, L. K. (1991). *Homeless families: Failed policies and young victims.* Washington, DC: Children's Defense Fund.

Miller, D. S. & Linn, E. H. B. (1988). Children in sheltered homeless families: Reported health status and use of health services. *Pediatrics, 81*, 668–673.

Neiman, L. (1988). A critical review of resiliency literature and its relevance to homeless children. *Children's Environments Quarterly, 5*(19), 17–25.

Palenski, J. E. & Launer, H. M. (1987). The "process" of running away: A redefinition. *Adolescence, 22*(86), 347–62.

Phillips, M., DeChillo, N., Kronenfeld, D., & Middleton–Jeter, V. (1988). Homeless families: Services make a difference. *Social Casework, 34*(1), 48–53.

Powers, J. L., Eckenrode, J., & Jaklitsch, B. (1988, March). *Running away from home: A response to adolescent maltreatment.* Paper presented at the Second Biennial Meeting of the Society for Research on Adolescence, Alexandria, VA. (ERIC Document Reproduction Service No. ED 296 228)

Rafferty, Y., & Rollins, N. (1989). *Learning in limbo: The educational deprivation of homeless children.* Long Island City, NY: Advocates for Children of New York.

Rafferty, Y., & Rollins, N. (1990, April). *Homeless children: Educational challenges for the 1990s.* Paper presented at the 98th Annual Convention of the American Psychological Association, Boston, MA. (ERIC Document Reproduction Service No. ED 325 589)

Rescoria, L., Parker, R., & Stolley, P. (1991). Ability, achievement and adjustment in homeless children. *American Journal of Orthopsychiatry, 61*(2), 210–220.

Rivlin, L. (1986). A new look at the homeless. *Social Policy, 16*(4), 3–10.

Rivlin, L. G. (1990). Home and homelessness in the lives of children. In N. A. Boxill (Ed.), *Homeless children: The watchers and the waiters* (pp. 5–17). Binghamton, NY: Haworth.

Rosenman, M., & Stein, M. L. (1990). Homeless children: A new vulnerability. In N. A. Boxill (Ed.), *Homeless children: The watchers and the waiters* (pp. 89–109). Binghamton, NY: Haworth.

Rossi, P. H. (1990). The old homeless and the new homelessness in historical perspective. *American Psychologist, 45*(8), 954–959.

Rowe, A. (1986, December). *Comprehensive plan for homeless families.* Washington, DC: Commission on Social Services, Department of Human Resources, District of Columbia Government.

Russell, S. C. & Williams, E. U. (1988). Homeless handicapped children: A special education perspective. *Children's Environments Quarterly*, 5(1), 3–7.

Schumack, S. (Ed.). (1987). *The educational rights of homeless children*. Cambridge, MA: Harvard University, Center for Law and Education. (ERIC Document Reproduction Service No. ED 288 915)

Stewart B. McKinney Homeless Assistance Act (P.L. 100–77). (July 22, 1987). Washington, DC: U.S. Government Printing Office.

Stewart B. McKinney Homeless Assistance Amendments Act of 1990 (P.L. 101-645). (Nov. 29, 1990). Washington, DC: U.S. Government Printing Office.

Stronge, J. H. & Helm, V. M. (1990, April). *Residency and guardianship requirements as barriers to the education of homeless children and youth*. Paper presented at the Annual Meeting of the American Educational Research Association, Boston, MA. (ERIC Document Reproduction Service No. ED 319 845)

Stronge, J. H., & Tenhouse, C. (1990). *Educating homeless children: Issues and answers*. Bloomington, IN: Phi Delta Kappa Educational Foundation.

Sullivan, P. A. & Damrosch, S. P. (1987). Homeless women and children. In R. Bingham, R. Green, & S. White (Eds.), *The homeless in contemporary society* (pp. 82–98). Newbury Park, CA: Sage.

Tower, C. C. & White, D. J. (1989). *Homeless students*. Washington, DC: National Education Association.

United States Conference of Mayors. (1989). *A status report on hunger and homelessness in America's cities: 1988*. (Available from U.S. Conference of Mayors, 1620 Eye Street, NW, Washington, DC 20006)

United States Department of Housing and Urban Development. (1989). *The 1988 national survey of shelters for the homeless*. Washington, DC: Author.

Wasem, R. E. (1989a). *Homelessness: Issues and legislation in the 101st congress* (CRS Publication No. IB88070). Washington, DC: Library of Congress.

Wasem, R. E. (1989b). *Programs benefiting the homeless: FY87–FY89 appropriations trends. CRS report for congress*. (Report No. CRS–89–20–EPW). Washington, DC: Congressional Research Service. (ERIC Document Reproduction Service No. ED 315 488)

Waxman, L. D. & Reyes, L. M. (1987). *A status report on homeless families in America's cities: A 29–city survey*. Washington, DC: U.S. Conference of Mayors. (ERIC Document Reproduction Service No. ED 296 018)

Weitzman, L. J. (1985). *The divorce revolution*. New York: Free Press.

Witt, V. (Ed.). (1988). *A children's defense budget: FY 1989. An analysis of our nation's investment in children.* (Report No. ISBN–0–938008–64–1). Washington, DC: Children's Defense Fund.

Women's Bureau. (1985). *The United Nations decade for women, 1976–1985: Employment in the United States.* Washington, DC: Department of Labor.

Wright, J. D. (1990). Homelessness is not healthy for children and other living things. In N. A. Boxill (Ed.), *Homeless children: The watchers and the waiters* (pp. 65–88). Binghamton, NY: Haworth.

Wright, J. D., & Lam, J. (1986). *The low–income housing supply and the problem of homelessness.* Amherst: University of Massachusetts, Social and Demographic Research Institute.

Resources

Organizations and Hotlines

Center for Law and Education
236 Massachusetts Avenue NE,
Suite 504
Washington, DC 20002
(202) 546–5300

Children's Defense Fund
122 C Street, NW
Fourth Floor
Washington, DC 20001
(202) 628-8787

Homelessness Information
Exchange
1830 Connecticut Avenue, NW
4th Floor
Washington, DC 20009
(202) 462–7551

Interagency Council on the
Homeless
451 Seventh Street, SW
Suite 7274
Washington, DC 20410
(202) 708-1480

Metro–Help/National Runaway
Switchboard
Lora Thomas
3080 N. Lincoln
Chicago, IL 60657
(312) 880–9860

National Coalition for the
Homeless
1621 Connecticut Avenue, NW
Fourth Floor
Washington, DC 20009
(202) 265-2371

National Governor's Association
444 North Capitol Street, NW
Suite 250
Washington, DC 20001
(202) 624-5300

National Resource Center for
Youth Services
Jim Walker/Peter Correia
University of Oklahoma
202 W. Eighth
Tulsa, OK 74119

National Volunteer
Clearinghouse for the Homeless
1310 Emerson Street, NW
Washington, DC 20011
(202) 722–2740

U.S. Department of Education
Education of Homeless
Children and Youth
400 Maryland Ave., SW, Room
4073
Washington, DC 20202
(202) 732–4682

State Coordinators for the Education of Homeless Children and Youth

State Contacts — Stewart B. McKinney Homeless Assistance Act

Alabama (AL)
Dr. Marsha Johnson
State Coordinator, Homeless Program
State Department of Education
Gordon Persons Building
50 North Ripley Street
Montgomery, Alabama
36130-3901
(205) 242-8199

Alaska (AK)
Ms. Connie Munro
Education Specialist
Department of Education
P.O. Box F
Juneau, Alaska 99811-0500
(907) 465-2970

Arizona (AZ)
Mr. Bill Scheel
Coordinator for Education of Homeless Children and Youth
Federal Programs Division
State Department of Education
1535 West Jefferson
Phoenix, Arizona 85007
(602) 542-5235

Arkansas (AR)
Ms. Paulette Mabry
Homeless Grant Coordinator, FPD
Arkansas Department of Education
State Education Building
4 State Capitol Mall
Little Rock, Arkansas 72201-1071
(501) 682-5761

California (CA)
Mr. James Spano
State Homeless Contact
State Department of Education
721 Capitol Mall
P.O. Box 944272
Sacramento, California
94244-2720
(916) 445-8235

Colorado (CO)
Ms. Mary Lou Myers
State Homeless Contact
Colorado Department of Education
201 East Colfax Avenue
Denver, Colorado 80203
(303) 866-8765

Connecticut (CT)
Ms. Hilary Freedman
Education for the Homeless
State Department of Education
25 Industrial Park Road
Middletown, Connecticut 06457
(203) 638-4272

Delaware (DE)
Mr. Jose Frank Soriano
State Specialist
ECIA Chapter 1, Migrant
Education
State Department of Public
Instruction
Townsend Building, P.O. Box
1402
Dover, Delaware 19901
(302) 739-4667

District of Columbia (DC)
Ms. Beverly Wallace
State Contact, Homeless
Program
District of Columbia Public
Schools
415 Twelfth Street, NW
Washington, DC 20004
(202) 576-8606

Florida (FL)
Mrs. Vessie Felton-Joseph
State Contact, Homeless
Program
State Department of Education
Knott Building (Collins L-34)
Tallahassee, Florida 32399
(904) 487-0017

Georgia (GA)
Mr. David Davidson
Project Manager
Program for Homeless Children
State Department of Education
1962 Twin Towers East
Atlanta, Georgia 30334
(404) 651-9328

Hawaii (HI)
Ms. Eloise Lee
State Contact, Homeless
Program
Student Personnel Services
Section
State Department of Education
1302 Queen Emma Street
Honolulu, Hawaii 96813
(808) 548-6079

Idaho (ID)
Ms. Anita Brunner
State Contact, Homeless
Program
State Department of Education
650 West State Street
Boise, Idaho 83720
(208) 334-2111

Illinois (IL)
Mr. John Edwards
State Contact, Homeless
Program
Chicago Regional Office
Illinois State Board of Education
100 West Randolph Street, Suite
14-300
Chicago, Illinois 60601
(312) 814-3606

Indiana (IN)
Mr. Harry Turner
State Contact, Homeless
Program
State Department of Education
State House, Room 229
Indianapolis, Indiana 46204-2798
(317) 232-0520

Iowa (IA)
Dr. Ray Morley
Bureau of Federal School
Improvement
State Department of Education
Grimes State Office Building
Des Moines, Iowa 50319-0146
(515) 281-5313

Kansas (KS)
Ms. Sandra Suttle
State Homeless Contact
State Department of Education
120 East 10th Street
Topeka, Kansas 66612
(913) 296-6066

Kentucky (KY)
Ms. Laura Graham
State Contact, Homeless
Program
State Department of Education
Capitol Plaza Tower, 17th Floor
Frankfort, Kentucky 40601
(502) 564-4201

Louisiana (LA)
Ms. Janet Langlois
State Contact, Homeless
Program
State Department of Education
654 Main Street
Baton Rouge, Louisiana 70801
(504) 342-3338

Maine (ME)
Mr. Frank J. Antonucci, Jr.
Consultant, Truancy, Dropout
& Alternative Education
Department of Educational and
Cultural Services
State House Station 23
Augusta, Maine 04333
(207) 289-5110

Maryland (MD)
Ms. Peggy Jackson-Jobe
Coordinator, Education of
Homeless Children and Youth
State Department of Education
200 West Baltimore Street, 4th
Floor
Baltimore, Maryland 21201
(301) 333-2445

Massachusetts (MA)
Ms. Lydia Macomber
Coordinator, Education of
Homeless Children and Youth
Department of Education
1385 Hancock Street
Quincy, Massachusetts 02169
(617) 770-7493

Michigan (MI)
Ms. Gloria Gordon
Office of School and
Community Affairs
Michigan Department of
Education
P.O. Box 30008
Lansing, Michigan 48909
(517) 373-6252

Minnesota (MN)
Ms. Barbara Yates
Coordinator, Education of
Homeless Children and Youth
State Department of Education
996 Capitol Square Building
550 Cedar Street
St. Paul, Minnesota 55101
(612) 296-3925

Mississippi (MS)
Ms. Cynthia Dorsey Smith
Coordinator, Education of
Homeless Children and Youth
State Department of Education
P.O. Box 771
Jackson, Mississippi 39205
(601) 359-3598

Missouri (MO)
Mr. Charlie Hungerford
Coordinator, Federal Programs
Department of Elementary &
Secondary Education
P.O. Box 480
Jefferson City, Missouri 65102
(314) 751-3805

Montana (MT)
Mr. Terry Teichrow
State Contact, Homeless
Program
Office of Public Instruction
State Capitol
Helena, Montana 59620
(406) 444-2036

Nebraska (NE)
Ms. Judy Klein
Coordinator of Education for
Homeless Children and Youth
State Department of Education
Post Office Box 94987
301 Centennial Mall South
Lincoln, Nebraska 68509
(402) 471-2478

Nevada (NV)
Ms. Holly Walton-Buchanan
State Coordinator for Homeless
Youth Program
State Department of Education
400 West King Street, Capitol
Complex
Carson City, Nevada 89710
(702) 687-3136

New Hampshire (NH)
Ms. Dorothy Schroepfer
State Contact, Homeless
Program
State Department of Education
101 Pleasant Street
Concord, New Hampshire 03301
(603) 271-2717

New Jersey (NJ)
Ms. Delia Georgedes
State Contact, Homeless
Program
State Department of Education
225 West State Street, CN 500
Trenton, New Jersey 08625
(609) 292-8777

New Mexico (NM)
Mr. Ralph Paiz
State Contact, Homeless
Program
State Department of Education
300 Don Gaspar
Santa Fe, New Mexico
87501-2786
(505) 827-6648

New York (NY)
Ms. Margretta R. Fairweather
Homeless Coordinator
State Education Department
99 Washington Avenue
EBA 362
Albany, New York 12234
(518) 474-5807

North Carolina (NC)
Mrs. Patricia Wilkins
Homeless Coordinator
State Department of Public
Instruction
116 West Edenton Street
Raleigh, North Carolina
27603-1712
(919) 733-0100

North Dakota (ND)
Mr. Robert Shubert
Program Planner, Education of
the Homeless
Department of Public Instruction
600 Boulevard East
Bismarck, North Dakota 58505
(701) 224-4646

Ohio (OH)
Mr. Jose Villa
Consultant, Homeless Education
Division of Federal Assistance
State Department of Education
933 High Street
Worthington, Ohio 43085
(614) 466-4161

Oklahoma (OK)
Mr. Keith Haley
Homeless Coordinator
State Department of Education
Oliver Hodge Memorial
Education Building
2500 North Lincoln Boulevard
Oklahoma City, Oklahoma
73105
(405) 521-3015

Oregon (OR)
Mr. Arnie Leppert
Director, Compensatory
Education
Oregon Department of
Education
700 Pringle Parkway SE
Salem, Oregon 97310
(503) 378-3606

Pennsylvania (PA)
Ms. Leslie Peters
Acting Coordinator, Office of
Education of Homeless Children
& Youth
Office of Policy and
Government Relations
Pennsylvania Department of
Education
333 Market Street, 10th Floor
Harrisburg, Pennsylvania
17126-0333
(717) 787-4605

Puerto Rico (PR)
Ms. Maria Emilia Pillot
State Contact, Homeless
Program
Department of Education
Post Office Box 759
Hato Rey, Puerto Rico 00919
(809) 754-0888

Rhode Island (RI)
Ms. Virginia Bilotti
State Contact, Homeless
Program
State Department of Education
22 Hayes Street
Providence, Rhode Island 02908
(401) 277-6523

South Carolina (SC)
Mr. J. C. Ballew
State Contact, Homeless
Program
Department of Education
1429 Senate Street, Room 1206
Columbia, South Carolina 29201
(803) 734-8327

South Dakota (SD)
Ms. Janet Ricketts
Coordinator for Homeless
Children, Youth, and Adults
Department of Education and
Cultural Affairs
700 Governors Drive
Pierre, South Dakota 57501
(605) 773-4437

Tennessee (TN)
Ms. Leslee Renner
State Contact, Homeless
Program
State Department of Education
135 Cordell Hull Building
Nashville, Tennessee 37219
(615) 741-6055

Texas (TX)
Ms. Barbara Wand
Director, Assistance to
Homeless Children
Texas Education Agency
1701 North Congress Avenue
Austin, Texas 78701
(512) 463-0694

Utah (UT)
Dr. Kenneth L. Hennefer
Project Coordinator, Services for
At Risk Students
State Office of Education
250 East 500 South Street
Salt Lake City, Utah 84111
(801) 538-7727

Vermont (VT)
Ms. Mary Elizabeth "Mitzi"
Beach
State Contact, Homeless
Program
State Department of Education
State Street
Montpelier, Vermont 05602-2703
(802) 828-2753 or (802) 658-6342

Virgina (VA)
Dr. Marie Spriggs-Jones
State Contact, Homeless
Program
State Department of Education
James Monroe Building, 23rd
Floor
Richmond, Virginia 23216
(804) 225-2910

Washington (WA)
Ms. Priscilla Scheldt
State Contact, Homeless
Program
Office of the Superintendent of
Public Instruction
Old Capitol Building, FG-11
Olympia, Washington 98504
(206) 753-3302

West Virginia (WV)
Mr. Robert Boggs
State Homeless Contact
State Department of Education
Capitol Complex, Room B-309
Charleston, West Virginia 25305
(304) 348-8830

Wisconsin (WI)
Mr. Paul Borowski
Consultant, Education for
Homeless Children and Youth
Department of Public Instruction
125 South Webster Street, Box
7841
Madison, Wisconsin 53707-7841
(608) 267-5153

Wyoming (WY)
Mr. Paul Soumokil
State Contact, Homeless
Children and Youth
State Department of Education
Hathaway Building
Cheyenne, Wyoming 82002
(307) 777-7168

American Samoa
Honorable Lealofi Viagalelai
Director of Education
Department of Education
Pago Pago, Tutuila 96799
(OS 684-633-5159)*

Guam (GU)
Honorable Anita A. Sukola
Director of Education
Department of Education
Post Office Box DE
Agana, Guam 96910
(OS 472-8901)*

Northern Mariana Islands
Mr. William P. Matson
Federal Programs Coordinator
Board of Education
Public School System
Commonwealth of Northern
Mariana Islands
P.O. Box 1370 CK
Saipan, MP 96950
(OS 933-9812)*

Virgin Islands (VI)
Mrs. Ida White
Homeless Coordinator
Department of Education
44-46 Kongens Gade
St. Thomas, Virgin Islands 00802
(809) 774-6505

Regional Coordinators on the Homeless

Ms. Lynda Baker
Regional Coordinator on the
Homeless
U.S. Department of Education
(Region I)
John W. McCormick Post Office
& Courthouse
Post Office Square
Boston, Massachusetts 02109
(617) 223-9317
FTS (8) 223-9317

Mr. Roland Alum
Regional Coordinator on the
Homeless
U.S. Department of Education
(Region II)
26 Federal Plaza, Room 36-118
New York, New York 10278
(212) 264-7008
FTS (8) 264-7005

---

*Overseas Operator

Ms. Kim Healay
Regional Commissioner on the Homeless
U.S. Department of Education
(Region III)
3535 Market Street, Room 16350
Philadelphia, Pennsylvania 19101
(215) 596-1001
FTS (8) 596-1001

Mr. John Lovegrove
Regional Coordinator on the Homeless
U.S. Department of Education
(Region IV)
P.O. Box 1777
Atlanta, Georgia 30301
(404) 331-2502
FTS (8) 223-9317

Mr. Brian Carey
Regional Coordinator on the Homeless
U.S. Department of Education
(Region V)
401 South State Street, Room 700-A
Chicago, Illinois 60605
(312) 353-5215
FTS (8) 353-7330

Ms. Dura Wilson
Regional Coordinator on the Homeless
U.S. Department of Education
(Region VI)
1200 Main Tower Building, Room 2125
Dallas, Texas 75202
(214) 767-3714
FTS (8) 729-3714

Mr. Donald Jacobsmeyer
Regional Coordinator on the Homeless
U.S. Department of Education
(Region VII)
10220 North Executive Hills Boulevard
P.O. Box 901381
Kansas City, Missouri 64190-1381
(816) 891-7972
FTS (8) 891-7972

Mr. David Ozman
Regional Coordinator on the Homeless
U.S. Department of Education
(Region VIII)
1961 Stout Street, Room 380
Denver, Colorado 80294
(303) 844-3544
FTS (8) 564-3544

Ms. Dorothy Vuksich
Regional Coordinator on the Homeless
U.S. Department of Education
(Region IX)
50 United Nations Plaza, Room 211
San Francisco, California 94102
(415) 556-4570
FTS (8) 556-4920

Mr. George Swift
Regional Coordinator on the Homeless
U.S. Department of Education
(Region X)
915 Second Avenue, Room 3362
Mail Code 10-9090
Seattle, Washington 98174-1099
(206) 442-0460
FTS (8) 399-0460

National Law Center on
Homelessness and Poverty
Ms. Lorraine Friedman
National Law Center on
Homelessness and Poverty
918 F Street, NW, Suite 412
Washington, DC 20004
(202) 638-2535

National Network of Runaway and Youth Services, Inc.

Della Hughes, Executive
Director
NNRYS
1400 I St., NW, Suite 330
Washington, DC 20005
(202) 682–4114

Regional Coordinators

Nancy Jackson
New England Consortium for
Families and Youth/Region I
Mass Committee for Children
and Youth
14 Beacon St., Suite 706
Boston, MA 02108
(617) 742–8555

Margo Hirsch
Empire State Coalition/Region II
121 Avenue of the Americas,
Room 507
New York, NY 10013
(212) 966–6477

Nancy Johnson
Mid–Atlantic Network of Youth
& Family Services/Region III
1168 Prince Andrew Ct.
Pittsburgh, PA 15237
(412) 366–6562

Gail Kurtz
Southeastern Network/Region
IV
337 S. Milledge, Suite 209
Athens, GA 30605
(404) 354–4568

Sara Jarvis
Southeastern Network/Region
IV
1019 W. Markham
Durham, NC 27701
(919) 687–4369

Barbara Rachaelson
MNRYS/Region V
115 W. Allegan, Suite 310
Lansing, MI 48933
(517) 484–5262

Theresa Andreas–Tod
TNOYS, SWNOYS/Region VI
406 West 40th St.
Austin, TX 78751
(512) 459–1455

Jack McClure, Chair
M.I.N.K./Region VII
P.O. Box 14403
Parkville, MO 64152
(816) 741–1477

Linda Wood
Mountain Plains Youth
Services/Region VIII
311 N. Washington
Bismarck, ND 58501

Nancy Fastenau
Western States Youth Services
Network/Region IX
1309 Ross St., Suite B
Petaluma, CA 94954
(707) 763–2213

Ginger Baggett
NW Network/Region X
94 Third St.
Ashland, OR 97520
(503) 482–8890

**State Networks/Coalitions
(Alphabetized by State)**

Darlene Dankowski
Crisis Residential Intervention
Services in Shelter
  (C.R.I.S.I.S)/Region IX
Open Inn, Inc.
4810 E. Broadway
Tucson, AZ 85711
(602) 323–0200

Andrea Bevernitz
Arkansas Youth Services
Providers Association /Region
VI
Youthbridge, Inc.
P.O. Box 668
Fayetteville, AR 72702
(501) 521–1532

Marilyn Ericksen
California Child, Youth and
Family Coalition
2424 Castro Way
Sacramento, CA 95818
(916) 739–6912

Tracy Kraft, Chair
CO Network of Runaway &
Homeless Youth
Services/Region VIII
c/o Gemini House
1629 Simms St.\Lakewood, CO
80215
(303) 235–0630

Bill Bentley
Florida Network of Youth &
Family Services/Region IV
804 E. Park Avenue
Tallahassee, FL 32301
(904) 222–4868

Sam Cox
Hawaii Youth Services
Network/Region IX
2006 McKinley St.
Honolulu, HI 96822
(808) 946–3635

Denis Murstein
IL Collaboration on
Youth/Youth Network
Council/Region V
506 S. Wabash Ave., Suite 510
Chicago, IL 60605
(312) 427–3247

Jim Killen
Indiana Youth Service
Association/Region V
2611 Waterfront Pkwy. East
Drive
Indianapolis, IN 46208
(317) 297–9639

Giles Gilliam
Louisiana Association of Child
Caring Agencies/Region VI
Harbour House
1146 Hodges
Lake Charles, LA 70601
(318) 432–1062

Sarah Baker, Director
Minnesota Association for
Runaway & Youth Services
9306 Country Club Rd. NE
Bemidji, MN 56601
(218) 751–8601

Elaine Mack–Jefferson
Garden State Coalition of Youth
& Family Concerns/Region II
514 E. State Street
Trenton, NJ 08609
(609) 393–4636

Gail Samuels
Nevada Alliance for
Children/Region IX
P.O. Box 1503
Crystal Bay, NV 89402
(702) 831–8978

Marg Elliston
New Mexico Youth Work
Alliance/Region VI
2801 Rodeo Rd., Suite B–538
Santa Fe., NM 87505
(505) 989–7424

Sally Maxton/Patricia Ellis
Ohio Youth Services
Network/Region V
50 W. Broad #320
Columbus, OH 43215
(614) 461–1354

Gay Phillips/Kathy Sutter
OK Association of Youth
Services/Region VI
National Resource Center for
Youth Services
202 W. Eighth St.
Tulsa, OK 74119
(918) 585–2986

Carol Kalgren
Youth Services Alliance of
PA/Region III
P.O. Box 1193
State College, PA 16801
(814) 237–5731

Shane Rock
TN Network of Youth & Family
Services
1617 16th Avenue South
Nashville, TN 37212
(615) 292–8255

Kathy Johnson
Vermont Coalition/Region I
c/o Washington County YSB
P.O. Box 627
Montpelier, VT 05602
(802) 229–9151

Peter Berliner
Alliance for Children Youth &
Families/Region X
172 – 20th Avenue
Seattle, WA 98122
(206) 324–0340

Pat Balke
WARS/Region V
2318 E. Dayton St.
Madison, WI 53704
(608) 241–2649

Tony Champaco/Sarah Thomas
Micronesian Youth Services
Network
c/o Sanctuary, Inc.
P.O. Box 21030, G.M.F.
Guam, M.I. 96921
011 (671) 734–2261 or 2537

CEC Mini-Library
Exceptional Children at Risk

A set of 11 books that provide practical strategies and interventions for children at risk.

- *Programming for Aggressive and Violent Students.* Richard L. Simpson, Brenda Smith Miles, Brenda L. Walker, Christina K. Ormsbee, & Joyce Anderson Downing. No. P350. 1991. 42 pages.

- *Abuse and Neglect of Exceptional Children.* Cynthia L. Warger with Stephanna Tewey & Marjorie Megivern. No. P351. 1991. 44 pages.

- *Special Health Care in the School.* Terry Heintz Caldwell, Barbara Sirvis, Ann Witt Todaro, & Debbie S. Accouloumre. No. P352. 1991. 56 pages.

- *Homeless and in Need of Special Education.* L. Juane Heflin & Kathryn Rudy. No. P353. 1991. 46 pages.

- *Hidden Youth: Dropouts from Special Education.* Donald L. Macmillan. No. P354. 1991. 37 pages.

- *Born Substance Exposed, Educationally Vulnerable.* Lisbeth J. Vincent, Marie Kanne Poulsen, Carol K. Cole, Geneva Woodruff, & Dan R. Griffith. No. P355. 1991. 28 pages.

- *Depression and Suicide: Special Education Students at Risk.* Eleanor C. Guetzloe. No. P356. 1991. 45 pages.

- *Language Minority Students with Disabilities.* Leonard M. Baca & Estella Almanza. No P357. 1991. 56 pages.

- *Alcohol and Other Drugs: Use, Abuse, and Disabilities.* Peter E. Leone. No. P358. 1991. 33 pages.

- *Rural, Exceptional, At Risk.* Doris Helge. No. P359. 1991. 48 pages.

- *Double Jeopardy: Pregnant and Parenting Youth in Special Education.* Lynne Muccigrosso, Marylou Scavarda, Ronda Simpson-Brown, & Barbara E. Thalacker. No. P360. 1991. 44 pages.

Save 10% by ordering the entire library, No. P361, 1991. Call for the most current price information, 703/620-3660.

Send orders to:
The Council for Exceptional Children, Dept. K11150
1920 Association Drive, Reston VA 22091-1589